RUTH LAW THRILLS A NATION

 *story and pictures by* **Don Brown**

Houghton Mifflin Company

Boston

Manufactured in the United States of America
Book design by David Saylor
The text of this book is set in 15 point Century Bold Condensed.
The illustrations are pen and ink and watercolor, reproduced in full color.

BVG   *10   9   8   7   6   5*

Library of Congress Cataloging-in-Publication Data

Brown, Don.
Ruth Law thrills a nation / by Don Brown.
p.   cm.
Summary: Describes the record-breaking flight of a daring woman
pilot, Ruth Law, from Chicago to New York in 1916.
RNF ISBN 0-395-66404-7   PAP ISBN 0-395-73517-3
1. Law, Ruth, 1887–1970 — Juvenile literature.   2. Air pilots —
United States — Biography — Juvenile literature.   3. Cross-country
flying — Juvenile literature.   [1. Law, Ruth, 1887–1970.   2. Air
pilots.   3. Women air pilots.   4. Cross-country flying.]   I. Title.
TL540.L273B76   1993
629.13'092 — dc20
[B]   92-45701   CIP   AC

To my father, who taught me about airplanes—and everything else

On November 19, 1916, Ruth Law tried to fly from Chicago to New York City in one day.

It had never been done before.

It was a frosty, blustery morning. Ruth woke up before dawn, but she did not feel the cold. To get used to the cold weather, she had slept in a tent on the roof of a Chicago hotel.

She put on two woolen suits,
one on top of the other.

Then she put on two leather suits

and covered her bulky outfit with a skirt.

In 1916, a polite lady *always* wore a skirt.

It was still dark when Ruth went to Grant Park on the Lake Michigan shore, where her plane was waiting. It was the tiny one she flew in air shows. Ruth called it a baby machine. It was good for stunts like loop-the-loop, but it was small and old. Ruth had tried to buy a newer, bigger plane for her long flight, but Mr. Curtiss, the manufacturer, had refused to sell her one. Hundreds of pilots had already been injured or killed flying, and Mr. Curtiss did not believe a woman could fly a large plane.

Mechanics had worked all night on the plane. They had attached a special windshield to protect Ruth from the cold wind, and had added a second gas tank so she would not have to stop for fuel more than once. Now the plane could carry fifty-three gallons of gasoline. But the additional gasoline made the plane too heavy. To get rid of some extra weight, the mechanics took the lights off the plane. Without them, Ruth would have to reach New York City before nightfall.

The freezing weather made the engine hard to start. More than an hour passed before Ruth could get under way.

At 7:20 A.M., Ruth climbed into the cockpit. She removed her skirt and stuffed it behind her seat—good sense defeated fashion.

She opened the throttle. The plane leaped forward and bounced over bumps and hollows. It raced awkwardly across the ground, then lifted toward the sky.

A fierce wind whipped through Chicago. It shook and tossed the small plane.

A dozen onlookers watched in fear.

A mechanic cried.

Ruth struggled to steady the plane as it dipped and pitched in the wind.

She narrowly topped the buildings and slowly climbed into the sky above Chicago. Ruth Law was on her way to New York City.

A mile above ground, Ruth sliced through the frigid winter air at one hundred miles an hour. She set her course by consulting the crude scroll of maps she had taped together and attached to her leg. She also had a compass, a clock, and a speedometer.

Ruth flew for nearly six hours. She was depending on the wind to help carry her from Chicago to New York City. But the wind died down. Only gasoline propelled the plane.

At approximately 2:00 P.M. eastern standard time, she neared Hornell, New York, where a group of supporters was waiting.

Then the engine quit.

The fuel tank was empty and Hornell was still two miles away.

The plane pitched slightly and sank. Ruth had only one chance to make a safe landing.

She struggled to control the steering gear. The field seemed to come up at her. The crowd of spectators spilled into her path. The plane brushed their heads.

Ruth was on the ground.

She was so cold and hungry that she had to be helped to a nearby car. She was driven to a restaurant for a lunch of scrambled eggs and coffee while her plane was refueled.

She had flown 590 miles nonstop. It was a record. No one in America had ever flown farther.

But Ruth's flight was not over.

At 3:24 P.M., Ruth set out again for New York City.

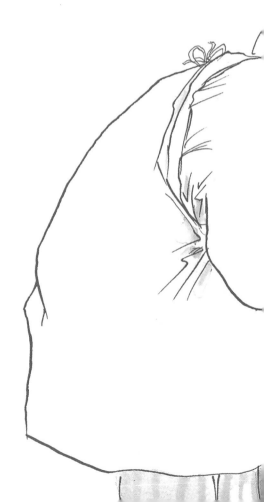

All day, newspapers told the story of Ruth's flight. A crowd in Binghamton, New York, had turned out, hoping to see her fly overhead. They were not disappointed. At first she was just a speck in the sky, but soon she made a striking cameo against the late afternoon sun.

Suddenly the plane slanted toward the ground and disappeared behind some trees.

"She's down! Something's broken!"

Nothing was broken. Ruth had decided to land. New York City was two hours away, but she would not be able to read her instruments in the dark. She tied the plane to a tree, wrapped her skirt around her, and accepted the hospitality of strangers.

The next morning, Ruth flew to New York City.

When she landed, an army general and a military band were there to greet her. Ruth was a heroine. "You beat them all!" the general said as he shook her hand.

Newspapers heralded her feat.

President Woodrow Wilson called her great.

A huge banquet was given in her honor.

On November 19, 1916, Ruth Law tried to fly from Chicago to New York City in one day and failed. Still, she set an American nonstop cross-country flying record—590 miles!—and thrilled a nation.

Her record stood for one year. It was broken by Katherine Stinson, another pilot who dared.